I0170169

Yoga

For

Flexibility

Monique Joiner Siedlak

OSHUN
PUBLICATIONS

Printed in the United States of America

Second Edition 2018

ISBN-13: 978-1-948834-58-2

Publisher
www.oshunpublications.com

Disclaimer
All the material contained in this book is provided for educational and informational purposes only. No responsibility can be taken for any results or outcomes resulting from the use of this material. While every attempt has been made to provide information that is both accurate and effective, the author does not assume any responsibility for the accuracy or use/misuse of this information.

Notice

This book is not intended as a substitute for the medical advice of physicians. The reader should regularly consult a physician or therapist in matters relating to his/her health and particularly with respect to any symptoms that may require diagnosis or medical attention.

Yoga Poses Photos

Pixabay.com

Freepik.com

Dreamstime.com

Cover Design by Monique Joiner Siedlak

Cover Image by Pixabay.com

Logo Design by Monique Joiner Siedlak

Logo Image by Pixabay.com

Sign up to email list: www.mojosiedlak.com

Other Books in the Series

Yoga for Beginners

Yoga for Stress

Yoga for Back Pain

Yoga for Weight Loss

Yoga for Advanced Beginners

Yoga for Fitness

Yoga for Runners

Yoga for Energy

Yoga for Your Sex Life

Yoga: To Beat Depression and Anxiety

Yoga for Menstruation

Table of Contents

Introduction i

Mountain Pose (Tadasana) 1

Tree Pose (Vrksasana) 6

Cat Pose (Marjariasana) 10

Cow Pose (Bitilasana) 14

Cobra Pose (Bhujangasana) 18

Locust Pose (Salabhasana) 22

Camel Pose (Ustrasana) 26

Bridge Pose (Setu Bandha Sarvangasana) 31

Chair Pose (Utkatasana) 35

Side Plank Pose (Vasisthasana) 39

Downward Facing Dog Pose (Adho Mukha
Svanasana) 43

Low Lunge Pose (Anjaneyasana) 47

High Lunge Pose (Utthita Ashwa Sanchalanasana)..51

Warrior Two Pose (Virabhadrasana II) 55

Warrior Three Pose (Virabhadrasana III).................59

Upward Facing Plank Pose (Purvottanasana)...........63

Eye of the Needle Pose (Sucirandhrasana) 67

Seated Forward Fold Pose (Paschimottanasana) 71

Legs up The Wall Pose (Viparita Karani).................75

Child's Pose (Balasana)...79

Corpse Pose (Shavasana) 83

Constructing a Yoga Sequence 87

About The Author 89

Other Books by Monique Joiner Siedlak 91

Connect With Me! 93

Introduction

When you ask people why they exercise, the most common answer would be to stay fit. Most people love to exercise because it uses their time positively and makes them feel good. Flexibility is not a common goal. People fail to realize how flexibility is a very important part of your health!

Flexibility can help relieve you of stress and anxiety, relieve of muscle pains and avoid injury. Yoga is a common way to increase flexibility. It is a common misconception that people have to be flexible to do yoga. That is not the case. In fact, the opposite of it is true.

There are three muscle groups where people are not as flexible as they should be. The hamstrings, hips, and shoulders. These muscles can tighten while sitting in the same position for a long time or excessive exercising. It is important when doing yoga for flexibility to not expect results in one day. Incorporate yoga exercises into your routine and you'll be on your merry way to a flexible and healthy body!

Mountain Pose (Tadasana)

The Mountain Pose can be employed as a resting pose or a preliminary pose for just about any standing asana. Even though this pose appears easy, it is great for improving your posture and body alignment, toning the spinal nerves, and creating a sense of consciousness throughout the body. As a pose in itself it's useful to practice. Simply stay in the pose for thirty seconds to one minute, breathing easily.

How to Do

Stand with the sides of your big toes coming into contact with each other. Your heels somewhat apart so that your second toes are matching. Elevate and expand your toes and the balls of your feet afterwards lay them gently down on the floor. Rock back and forth and side to side. Bit by bit decrease this move to and fro to a standstill, with your weight steadied equally on your feet.

Secure your thigh muscles and raise the kneecaps, without strengthening your lower belly. Raise the inside ankles to build up the inside arches. Begin to visualize a line of energy all the way up along your inner thighs to your groins, and from there through the core of your torso, neck, and head, and out through the top of your head. Turn the upper thighs somewhat inward. Elongate your tailbone in the direction of the floor and raise the pubis to the navel.

Pressing your shoulder blades into your back, broaden them crossways and drop them down towards your back. Without moving forward your lower front ribs, raise the top of your sternum straight toward the ceiling. Extend your collarbones, hanging your arms alongside your torso.

Square the top of your head straight over the middle of your pelvis, with the bottom of your chin parallel to the floor, throat soft, and the tongue wide and flat on the floor of your mouth. Soften your eyes.

Benefits

Improves posture, strengthens abdomen and buttocks. Can relieve back pain and decreases flat feet.

Tips

Use a block in the middle of the thighs. The block should be rotated so that the short end looks towards the front. With your legs, squeeze the block and roll it somewhat backward to feel the meeting and turning of the thighs. Take a number of breaths this way.

Then remove the block but replicate the action of your thighs as is the block was there. You don't have to use the block every time, but it helps to remember what rolling it back felt like.

Tree Pose (Vrksasana)

Tree Pose is a yoga pose that will aid you in increasing your stability and mental focus. It could also help you build up the muscles in your legs and core. The lower body offers the assistance for the upper body in this pose.

How to Do

Following the Mountain Pose, bend your left knee transferring all the weight into your right leg. Afterward, direct the left knee to the left wall placing the heel at the side of the right leg.

Look towards the floor and focus at one point. Gradually move as high up as you can maintain your balance, your left foot up the right leg. Once you are balanced at this point, slowly bring the palms together, in a prayer posture in front of your heart.

Keep on focusing at your focal point on the floor. Keeping your right leg forcefully pressing your foot into the floor, maintain your left knee bent ninety degrees towards the side wall. Your shoulders should be down with your back and the chest is pushing forward.

If you are extremely balanced at this point, take a crack at the next phase by breathing in and raising your arms over your head. The arms begin in the football field goal position. You can place your palms together with the thumbs intersected, or your fingers can be intertwined with the index finger pointed up. The fingers are reaching up and the shoulders are down and back.

Breathe and hold for five to ten breaths. To release, slowly exhale the arms down and then release the legs back into the Mountain Pose. Repeat this pose on the other side.

Benefits

The Tree Pose increases balance, memory, concentration, and focus, as well as strengthening the ankles and knees. The Tree Pose extends the groin, torso thighs, and shoulders. It tones your abdominal muscles and develops strength in your calves. This pose also helps to improve flat feet and is beneficial for back trouble.

Tips

First off, take your time. Carefully go through the directions for the Mountain Pose before performing the Tree Pose. It offers the physical basis for this pose.

Stabilize your weight completely throughout your standing foot Attain the position in your hips, tailbone, pelvis, and abdomen; followed by in your collarbones, shoulder blades, arms, and neck. Lengthen the pose through the top of your head. Once you are prepared, you can then lift your arms in the air.

At no time should you lay the foot of your elevated leg completely on your knee or on the side of your knee joint.

Even though the consistent practice of the Tree Pose will tone up the abdominal muscles, your weaker abdominal muscles can cause it challenging to balance.

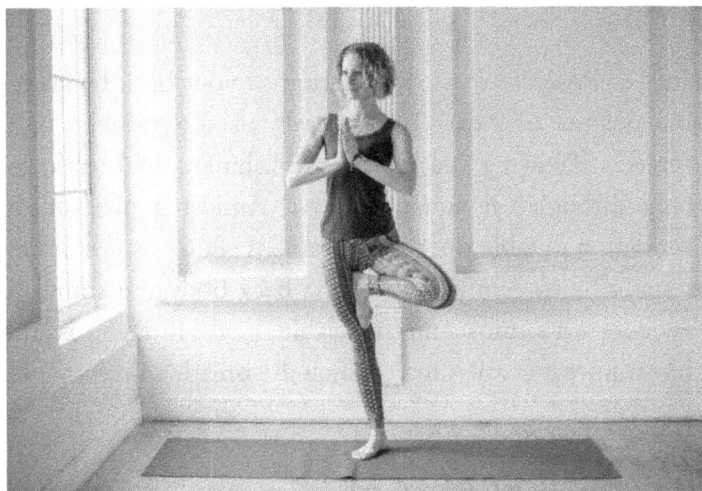

Cat Pose (Marjariasana)

The Cat Pose consists of relaxation of your back by taking on a posture of a cat. It is generally used to begin a yoga exercise, following the initial establishment of breath, by going through cat and cow pose. Amidst a nice steady foundation in tabletop, this movement allows us grounding as we begin to gently open up the back body and stimulate the core. It's most indispensable goal, though, is the opportunity it enables to combine the breath with activity.

How to Do

Start off by placing yourself in a tabletop position, using your hands and knees as the four legs of a table. Your knees would be positioned up and down below your hips. Your shoulders, wrists, and elbows should be parallel and perpendicular to the ground. You will then focus your eyes on the floor, with your head in a middle position.

Let your breath out and allow your spine to curve by directing it upward to the ceiling. Your shoulders and knees should be in the recommended four-legged position.

At this moment, let your head somewhat fall towards the floor. Do not fall so far that your chin is pressed into the sternal hollow of your chest.

While inhaling, once again come back to the typical tabletop position. Maintain breathing in and breathing out deeply while transferring your position from relaxed to alert. Maintain until you feel the relaxation in your spine.

Benefits

The Cat Pose gradually works your spine as well as its muscles. It stretches your neck, back, and torso. In addition to improving the functions of your belly organs, it calms your mind by alleviating it from tension and stress.

Tip

The Cat Pose is an easy and simple yoga pose to relax your fatigued body. Ask your partner or friend to lay a hand in the middle of your shoulder blades if you are finding it challenging to bring a curve in the upper section of your back which will then result in a prompt triggering of that area.

Cow Pose (Bitilasana)

The Cow Pose is regularly instructed in sequence with the Cat Pose to do a mild warm-up sequence. When practiced together, the poses help to stretch the body and prepare it for other activity.

You will inhale through the Cow Pose and exhale through the Cat Pose.

How to Do

Begin with your hands and knees in a tabletop position. You should make sure you align your shoulders above your wrists and your hips are aligned above your knees. Come to a horizontal back by lengthening the spine. Place your head and neck in a non-aligned position, staring down in the direction of the floor.

Breathe in and curve your back. Elevate through your glutes and the crown of your head and allow your belly to drop toward the floor. Rotate the shoulders up and down the back, feeling the back bend in your thoracic spine. Widen up your chest.

Hold the Cow Pose for one breath. Exhale and come back to a nonaligned, tabletop position again. You can also practice this in combination with the Cat Pose, alternating inhales with the Cow Pose and exhales with the Cat Pose.

Benefits

This is a gentle backbend that works with the Cat Pose to awaken the spine. Opens the chest, shoulders and upper back. Teaches the connection between inhaling and expanding and exhaling and contracting.

Tip

Care for your neck by widening your shoulder blades and pulling your shoulders down, away from your ears.

Cobra Pose (Bhujangasana)

The Cobra Pose is a familiar Yoga backbend. When you perform the Cobra Pose, you stretch the front of your torso and spine.

How to Do

Lie face down on the floor. Extend your legs back, with the tops of your feet on the floor. Stretch your hands on the floor beneath your shoulders. Squeeze the elbows back into your body. Push the tops of your feet, thighs, and pubis powerfully into the floor.

On an inhalation, start to straighten your arms to raise your chest off the floor. Go only to a height at which you can sustain a connection throughout your pubis to your legs. Press your tailbone toward the pubis and raise the pubis toward your navel. Narrow the hip, compressing but don't harden your buttocks.

Firm the shoulder blades against the back, puffing the side ribs forward. Lift through the top of the sternum but avoid pushing the front ribs forward, which only hardens the lower back. Distribute the backbend evenly throughout the full spine.

Hold the pose anywhere from fifteen to thirty seconds, breathing freely. Release back to the floor with an exhalation.

Benefits

The Cobra Pose is best known for its capability to build up the flexibility of your spine. It stretches the chest along with strengthening your spine and shoulders. It further assists in opening the lungs and stimulating the abdominal organs, improving digestion.

An energizing backbend, the Cobra Pose can reduce stress and fatigue. It also firms and tones the shoulders, abdomen, and buttocks, and assists in easing back pain.

Tip

The Cobra Pose will be able to energize and warm up the body, getting it ready for the deeper backbends in your yoga routine.

Locust Pose (Salabhasana)

The Locust Pose is a transitional backbend that strengthens and tones the whole back of your body.

How to Do

Lying prone (on your stomach), push your chin against the mat. Keeping your hands in fists with thumbs inside, put your straight arms beneath your thighs. Extend your legs straight behind you, hip-width apart. Make an effort with your back muscles and supporting with your fists from below, use your inner thighs to lift your legs up toward the ceiling, raising both your legs up. Keep this position without holding your breath.

Benefits

The Locust Pose opens your shoulders and neck while it strengthens the back and abdomen. It also eases upper-back aches.

Tip

Roll a blanket and position it at the bottom of your rib cage if you're not gaining much lift in your chest. Practicing like this way will help you strengthen your back muscles.

Camel Pose (Ustrasana)

The Camel Pose is an intermediate level back-bending yoga. This yoga posture adds flexibility and strength to the body and also helps in improving digestion.

How to Do

Kneeling on the floor, place your knees hip-width apart and set your hips over the knees. Use a folded blanket if your knees or ankles have aches due to the floor to kneel on. Ground the pose by slightly pushing the top of your feet into the floor.

Lightly tighten your lower abdomen to lean your tailbone down; this will draw your hip points somewhat up towards the bottom of your front ribs. Avoid having stiffness in your buttocks and outer hips while holding this pelvic tilt.

As you maintain a light steadiness in your abdomen, set your hands on the back of your pelvis. The bottom of your palms should go across the tops of your buttocks allowing your fingers to point down. Urge your lower back to lengthen as your tailbone moves deeper into a pelvic tilt as though it is drawing forward toward your pubis. In the course of this action, you should also feel your bottom front ribs slightly being contained as a result adding to the length through your lower back.

Continuing into the back arch, breathe in and roll your shoulders back by pressing your shoulder blades back and against your back ribs. Your chest will inflate and lift. Maintain your pelvis forward over your knees and somewhat lean back against the firmness of the tailbone and shoulder blades.

Remain in this only if you feel relaxed and strong, by slightly twisting to one side to smoothly place one hand on the back of the one heel. Return the spine to center to place the other hand on the other heel. Still keeping the firmness and energy in the abdomen, gently press your thighs forward to perpendicular if the hips have moved back relative to the knees.

Lightly contain the bottom front ribs and continue to lift your hip points towards those ribs to reduce compression of your lower back. Your hands may be positioned so that your palms are on the heels and the fingers point over the soles of the feet. This will allow your upper arm to more effectively externally rotate and add to the expansion of your shoulders and chest. You can continue the pose with the gaze forward. A more advanced version, you can relax the neck and jaw as you gently float your head back. Relax and soften your throat as much as possible-opening the mouth will reduce muscle tension in the front of the neck. Hold the pose with comfort and ease of breath for twenty seconds to a minute.

To release this pose, breathe out and tighten your abdominal muscles. Little by little bring your hands on top of the back of your pelvis one at a time. As you breathe in, tighten your abdominal muscles more to pull your bottom ribs forward causing your trunk to flex forward. Continue to lift your chest over your knees. If your head is back, wait for your chest pass over your knees. At that point let your head flow forward with gravity to avoid strain to the neck. Move slowly into the Child's Pose and rest for a few breaths taking breaths deep into your back.

Benefits

The Camel Pose stretches the front of your body, for the most part, the abdomen, chest, quadriceps, and hip flexors. It improves your spinal flexibility, at the same time as also strengthening your back muscles and improving your posture.

Tip

Beginners very frequently aren't capable to touch their hands to their feet without injuring their back or even their neck. To start with, attempt to turn your toes under and raise your heels. Follow by resting each hand on a block.

Place the blocks just outside each heel, and position them at their highest height. If you're still experiencing difficulty, obtain a chair. Kneel for the pose with your back to the chair, with your calves and feet beneath the seat and the front edge of the seat touching your buttocks. Afterward lean back and bring your hands to the sides of the seat or high up on the front chair legs.

You can also to place a cushion under your knees to assist your way into the pose.

Bridge Pose (Setu Bandha Sarvangasana)

The Bridge Pose is a beginning backbend that helps to open your chest and stretch your thighs.

How to Do

To begin, lie supine (on your back). Fold your knees and keep your feet hip distance apart on the floor, ten to twelve inches from your pelvis, with your knees and ankles in a straight line. With your arms beside your body, place your palms faced down.

Breathe in, while slowly lifting your lower back, middle back and upper back off the floor. Gently roll in your shoulders. Touch your chest to your chin without bringing the chin down. Support your weight with your shoulders, arms, and feet. Feel your buttocks firm up in this pose. Both your thighs should be parallel to each other and to the floor.

You could interlock your fingers and push your hands on the floor to lift your torso a bit more up if you want or you could support your back with your palms. Keep breathing easily. Hold this pose for a minute or two and then exhale as you gently release the pose.

Benefits

The Bridge Pose strengthens your back, opens the chest, and improves your spinal mobility.

Tips

After you roll your shoulders under, be sure not to pull them away from your ears. This often overstrains your neck. Raise the tops of your shoulders toward your ears and push your inner shoulder blades away from your spine.

Chair Pose (Utkatasana)

The Chair Pose is a standing yoga posture that tones your entire body. The Chair Pose is an important component of Sun Salutations and is also often used as a transitional pose. It can also be practiced on its own to help build strength and stamina through your entire body.

How to Do

Begin with the Mountain Pose. Your big toes should be in contact of each other and your heels should be fixed a little apart. Your lower belly has to be drawn in a little to help support your spine. Move your shoulder blades downward keep your chest open and pushed out across your shoulders.

Take a deep breath and raise your arms over your head. You can keep your arms parallel to each other or just keep them up with the palms joined, facing inward. Your arms should be held at the same height or in front of your ears.

Bring your lower ribs toward your pelvis. At that point, breathe out and bend your knees. Try to make your thighs as parallel to the floor as you can. Your knees should come out in front of your feet. The torso should lean a little forward over the thighs till the torso makes a right angle with the upper part of the thighs. Your inner thighs should be parallel to each other and they should push the tops of your thigh bones to the heels.

Keep the edges of your shoulders firm. Bring your tailbone downward to the ground and towards your pubic bone to extend your lower back.

Remain in this pose for thirty seconds to one minute. To release, straighten your knees while you breathe in. Afterward, breathe out and bring your arms to the sides of your body, back into the Mountain Pose.

Benefits

The Chair pose exercises the spine, hips and chest muscles. It also helps to strengthen the lower back, torso and toning the thigh, ankle, leg and knee muscles.

Tips

Practice this near a wall to help you remain in the pose. You can stand with your back near the wall just a few inches away from it. Keep a proper distance to when you come into position, your tailbone comes into contact it then supported by the wall.

Side Plank Pose (Vasisthasana)

The Side Plank Pose is a balancing pose requires focus and determination to practice, in addition to a strong understanding of the basis of the pose. It's a great way to develop not only your shoulder and wrist strength but also your core and leg strength.

How to Do

Begin in the Downward Facing Dog Pose. Move onto the outside edge of your left foot, and stack your right foot on top of your left foot.

Walk your left hand slightly forward and bring your right hand to your right hip, stacking your right side body over your left side body so that you face the right side of your area. Your body should form one straight diagonal line from the top of your head to your feet.

Dig into the knuckle of your index finger and thumb on your left hand to alleviate the pressure on your wrist, and then steady your left arm, rotating the bicep of your arm forward and the triceps backward.

Keep your right hand on your hip, or extend your hand up towards the ceiling and let your eyes look turn upwards too.

Hold here for fifteen to thirty seconds, at that time come back to the Downward Facing Dog and repeat on the other side, holding for the same length of time as with the other side.

Benefits

The Side Plank Pose strengthens the abdomen, arms, wrists and legs. It also improves your balance.

Tip

Instead of stacking your feet on top of each other, just leave your feet where they were in your plank as you rotate open to the side to make balance easier. The foot of your top leg will end up in front of your other foot, providing you a more solid support. You can also rest your lower knee on the floor to make it easier to hold this pose.

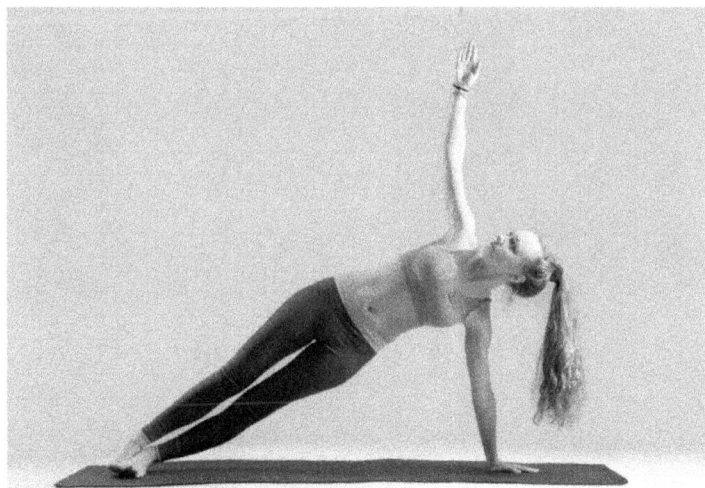

Downward Facing Dog Pose (Adho Mukha Svanasana)

Downward Facing Dog Pose is one of the traditional Sun Salutation sequences poses. It's also an excellent yoga asana all on its own.

How to Do

Begin with your hands and knees in a tabletop position. Make sure your shoulders are aligned above your wrists and your hips are aligned above your knees. Come to a flat back by lengthening the spine. Place your head and neck in a non-aligned position, staring down in the direction of the floor.

Breathe out and raise your knees away from the floor. At the start, keep your knees slightly bent and your heels lifted away from the floor. Lengthen your tailbone positioned from the back of your pelvis and press it slightly toward the pubis. Alongside this tension, raise the resting bones in the direction of the ceiling, and from your inner ankles pull the inner legs up into the groin.

Followed by letting your breath out, push your top thighs back and extend your heels against or down toward the floor. Making sure that you do not lock them, straighten your knees and steady your outer thighs, rolling the upper thighs inward slightly, narrowing the front of the pelvis.

Firming the outer arms, press the bottoms of your index fingers assertively into the floor. From these two points, lift alongside the inside of your arms from the wrists to the tops of the shoulders. Firm your shoulder blades against your back then widen them and draw them toward the tailbone. Keep your head between your upper arms; not allowing it to simply hang.

Continue in this pose somewhere between one to three minutes. Afterward, bend your knees to the floor with a breath and repose in the Child's Pose.

Benefits

Downward Facing Dog pose can help decrease back pain through strengthening the whole back and shoulder girdle. It aids in stronger hands, wrists, the Achilles tendon, low-back, hamstrings, and calves, as well as increasing the full-body circulation. Elongates your shoulders and shoulder blade area. Decrease in tension and headaches by elongating the cervical spine and neck and relaxing the head. It can also lessen anxiety and expand your respiration

Tip

You can alleviate the burden on your wrists by employing a block beneath your palms or you can be capable of completing the pose upon your elbows. By lifting your hands on blocks or the seat of a chair, you can help to release and open your shoulders.

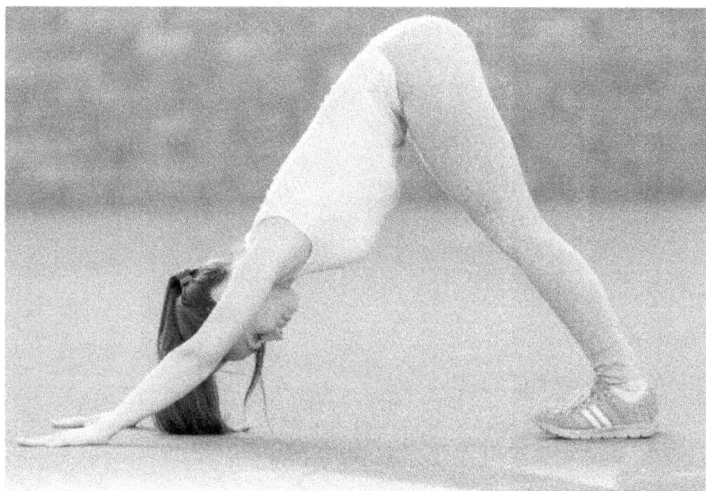

Low Lunge Pose (Anjaneyasana)

The Low Lunge Pose is a simple standing pose that stretches and strengthens your entire body. The Low Lunge is suitable for all levels from pre-natal to the advanced styles of yoga. Runners will, for the most part, welcome the strong stretch in the hamstrings and hip flexors.

How to Do

Begin in the Downward Facing Dog Pose. On an exhalation, step your left foot forward and place it beside your left thumb, lining up your left knee over your left ankle. Lower your right knee to the floor, ensuring to place it behind your hips.

On an inhalation, bring up your torso and stretch your arms above your head with your palms facing each other, placing your biceps at the sides of your ears. On your following exhale, let your hips to descend forward and down until you feel extent in the front of your left leg and psoas (the core of your body).

Draw your tailbone downward to the, lengthening your lower back and engaging your core muscles. Begin to draw your thumbs into the backplane of your body as you reach up with your heart, and shift your gaze up for a mild backbend. Remain here, or you can raise your back knee off the mat for the Crescent Lunge Pose.

To leave this pose, set your hands down on the mat and move back to the Downward Facing Dog Pose. Repeat with the right leg forward.

Benefits

The Low Lunge pose is an excellent pose to stretch out your tight quadriceps, hamstrings, groin, and hips. It also assists in a full range of motion in your lower body. This pose is ideal for cyclists, runners, and individuals who sit all day at desks.

Tip

Practice this pose facing a wall to improve balance. Push your big toe of the front foot against the wall and extend your arms up with your fingertips to the wall.

High Lunge Pose (Utthita Ashwa Sanchalanasana)

The High Lunge Pose is a standing pose that is applicable for all levels and styles of yoga. The High Lunge is typically practiced at the beginning of a series as part of a salute sequence or warm-up. It elongates and builds up your back, shoulders and leg muscles.

How to Do

Starting in the Table Pose (on your hands and knees), step your left foot forward between your two hands, with the knee directly over the ankle. Tuck your back toes under and straighten the back leg. Press the palms, fingers or fists into the floor to raise the top of your head up towards the ceiling.

Move your shoulders down and back pressing your chest forward. Look straight ahead with your chin parallel to the floor. Extend your back leg by pushing the heel in the direction of the floor and by pressing the back of your knee up in the direction of the ceiling. Relax your hips and allow them to descend down towards the floor. Breathe and hold for two to six breaths.

To release from this pose, lower your right knee down and slide the left knee back into the Table pose, or step the left foot going back to the Downward Facing Dog. Repeat on the other side.

Benefits

The High Lunge Pose opens the top of your thighs and develops leg strength.

Tip

Fix a block in the middle of the floor and your back leg to keep this pose longer.

Warrior Two Pose (Virabhadrasana II)

The Warrior Two Pose is the second of a sequence of three yoga poses that improve strength and stamina.

How to Do

From the Downward Facing Dog, step your left foot to the inside your left hand. Bend your left knee over your ankle so your thigh is parallel to the floor. Swivel on the ball of your right foot to bring your right heel to your mat. Your right foot should be at a 90-degree angle with the sole planted.

Your front heel is lined up with your back arch. Rise to stand. Open your hips to the right side of your mat. Your torso will face right. Extend your left arm toward the front of the mat and your right arm toward the back of the mat with your palms facing down. Keep both arms parallel to the floor. Release your shoulders away from your ears. Reach out through the fingertips of both hands.

Turn your head to face the front of your mat. Your gaze is forward over the left hand. Both thighs are rotating outward. Engage your triceps to support your arms, your quadriceps to support your legs, and your belly to support your torso.

After several breaths, windmill your hands down to either side of your left foot and step back to Downward Dog. Stay here for a few breaths or go through a transition before repeating the pose with the right foot forward.

Benefits

Tones the abdomen, strengthen your legs and arms and opens your chest and shoulders.

Tips

When you bend the right knee to a right angle, bend it with a meaningful exhalation, and point the inside the right knee in the direction of the little-toe side of the right foot.

Warrior Three Pose (Virabhadrasana III)

The Warrior Three Pose is an intermediate balancing pose in yoga. This energetic standing posture builds stability throughout your whole body by incorporating all of the muscles through your core, arms, and legs.

How to Do

Begin in the Mountain Pose. With an exhale, move your right foot back about two feet, as you maintain your body weight forward on your left foot. Keep your left toes looking forward. Feel your left toes spread and find an even basis through the sole of your left foot. Put your hands on your hips to bring into line your hips and shoulders perpendicular to the front of your mat. Tighten your inner core muscles by pulling in the navel and waist.

Maintain a feeling you are holding the lower organs with a round band of muscle, then breathe in and raise your right foot as your incline your torso forward experiencing a hinging movement at your hips. Direct your stare straight down as you bend forward from your hips attaining a new focus.

As your torso and right leg go into a corresponding position with the floor, lengthen both legs without bracing into the bottom knee. The right hip may rise higher than the left. Keeping your right hip level with the left hip, experience a shift in a correct postural alignment. Imagine more length advancing into the right leg and spine. Maintain the digging into the left foot and tightening into the core muscles.

To intensify the influence of the balance, free your hands from your hips and elongate your arms straight out to the sides expanding your chest or forward in line with your head and neck. If you extend your arms forward, then turn your palms to face each other so your shoulder blades can draw down away from your ears. Breathe and stay here for five to ten breaths.

To release this pose, inhale as you lift your chest and place your right foot back into Mountain Pose. Exhale as you lower your arms, and draw a few breaths as you pause and then repeat on the right side for the same time.

Benefits

The Warrior III pose strengthens your legs, improves balance and your core strength.

Tip

You can either stand in front of the wall, bringing your arms outstretched in front of you with your hands on the wall or rotate and bring the raised back foot onto the wall. Both will give you the stability you require to level your hips. You can also hold on a chair as a substitute for using the wall.

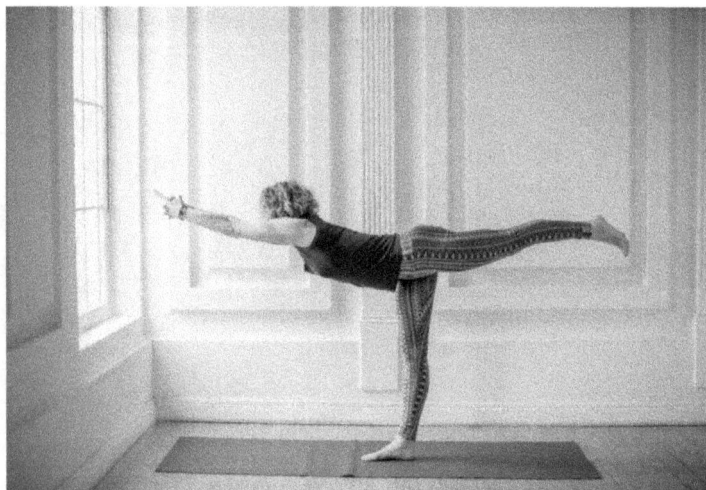

Upward Facing Plank Pose
(Purvottanasana)

The Upward Plank Pose is a deep stretch across the front of the body.

How to Do Begin Perform

In the Staff Pose, place your hands several inches behind your hips with your fingertips facing forwards towards your feet. Bring down your knees and arrange your feet on the floor at hip width apart. With an exhalation, press through your hands and feet to lift your hips to the same height as your shoulders and straighten your arms. Engage your core muscles as you slowly straighten one leg at a time and point your toes. Engage your pelvic floor and raise your hips as high as you can. Keep your legs strong and your glutes firm. Roll your shoulders onto your back and lift your chest. Being mindful of your neck, let your head hang back behind you. Hold this pose for up to thirty seconds, afterwards slowly sit back down.

Benefits

The Upward Plank pose Opens the chest, stretches your shoulders, wrists and ankles, as well as strengthening your arms, legs and back.

Tips

Using a chair for support sit near the front side of the seat and wrap your hands around the back edge. Inhale to raise your pelvis and then extend each leg with an inhale.

Eye of the Needle Pose
(Sucirandhrasana)

The Eye of the Needle is a lying-down yoga pose that gets rid of rigidity in the outer hips and lower back. If you pass a great deal of time sitting, those muscles grow tight and short as a result of the lack of use.

How to Do

Start by reclining on your back with your knees bent and the bottom of your feet on the floor. Clasp your right knee into your chest. Cross the right ankle over your body and place it on the left thigh. Let the right knee relax away from your chest.

Raise your left foot off the floor and thread your right hand through your legs, which creates the eye of the needle, so that your hands come together on the back side of your left thigh. You can also, hold your hands on the front side of your left shin. Using your hands, pull your left thigh toward your chest. This will trigger your right hip to open. Keep both of your feet stretched. Breathe deeply and relax the right knee to open the hips.

Repeat on the other side.

Benefits

The Eye of the Needle stretches lower back opens hips reduces back pain.

Tip

The more you push your knee back, the more your hips will open and the deeper the stretch will be down the legs. If it feels painful because the stretch is too deep, angle your knee in the direction of your upper body. Use a yoga strap, tie or scarf by circling it around the back of the thigh and gripping each end with one hand, if you are unable to clasp your hands around your thigh.

Seated Forward Fold Pose
(Paschimottanasana)

The Seated Forward Fold is a calming yoga pose that aids to relieve stress. This pose is frequently performed later in a series, when the body is warm.

How to Do

From the Staff Pose, inhale the arms up over the head and lift and lengthen up through the fingers and crown of the head. Exhale and bend at the hips, slowly drop your torso towards your legs. Reach the hands to the toes, feet or ankles.

To deepen the stretch, use the arms to gently pull the head and torso closer to the legs. Press out through the heels and gently draw the toes towards you. Breathe and hold for five to ten breaths. To release from this pose slowly roll up the spine back into Staff pose. Inhale the arms back over your head as you lift the torso back into the Staff pose.

Benefits

The Seated Forward Fold delivers a deep stretch for the whole back side of your body from the heels to the neck. The Forward Fold soothes your nervous system and emotions.

Tips

By no means should force yourself into a forward bend, particularly when sitting on the floor. Extend forward, when you feel the area between your pubis and navel shortening, you should stop, lift up a little, and lengthen again. Frequently, because of the tightness in the backs of your legs, a beginner's forward bend doesn't go very far forward and may possibly look more like sitting up straight.

Legs up The Wall Pose (Viparita Karani)

The Legs up the Wall Pose is an upturn pose where you lie on the floor against a wall and position your legs together vertically against the wall.

How to Do

If you are performing the assisted version, place a firm pillow or cushion on the floor against the wall.

Start off the pose by sitting with your right side against the wall. Your lower back should rest against the bolster if you're using one. Slightly turn your body to the right and bring your legs up onto the wall. On the other hand, if you are using a pillow, shift your lower back onto it before bringing your legs up the wall. Use your hands for balance as you transfer your weight.

Drop your back to the floor and lie down. Relax your shoulders and head on the floor. Transfer your weight from side-to-side and move your buttocks close to the wall. Allow your arms to rest open at your sides with your palms facing up. If you're using a pillow, your lower back should at this time be totally held by it.

Allow the part of your bone that connects in the hip socket (the top of your thigh bones) to release and relax, dropping in the direction of the back of your pelvis.

Close your eyes and hold for five to ten minutes, as you breathe with mindfulness.

To release, slowly boost yourself away from the wall and slide your legs down to the left side. Use your hands to help press yourself back up into a seated position.

Benefits

This pose reduces fatigue, cramping in the legs and feet and stretches the back of the legs. It can be an excellent pose for alleviating swollen ankles and calves triggered by long periods of standing pregnancy, and travel. It furthermore elongates the front of the upper body as well as the back of the neck and can be helpful for relieving mild backaches.

Tips

Use your breath to ground the tops of your thighs bones into the wall, which assists in the release of your abdomen, spine, and groins. Imagine in the pose, which each inhalation is falling through your upper body and pushing the tops of your thigh bones closer to the wall. Next with each exhale, hold your thighs to the wall and let your upper body extend over the bolster away from the wall and onto the floor.

Child's Pose (Balasana)

The Child's Pose is a popular beginner's yoga posture. It is generally utilized as a resting position in among more difficult poses throughout a yoga practice.

How to Do

Come to all fours (Table Pose) exhale and lower your hips to your heels and forehead to the floor. Kneeling on the floor, bring your big toes together and sit on your heels, then separate your knees about as far as your hips.

Your arms can be above your head with your palms on the floor. Your palms can be flat or fisted with them stacked under your forehead, or your arms can be at the sides of your body with your palms up.

The Child's Pose is a resting pose. Remain in this position anywhere from thirty seconds to a few minutes. Beginners can also use this pose to get a feel of a deep forward bend. To come up, first stretch your front torso, followed by an inhalation lift from your tailbone as it pushes down and into your pelvis.

Benefits

The Child's Pose aids to stretch your hips, thighs, and ankles at the same time it reduces stress and fatigue. It gradually relaxes the muscles on the front of your body while softly and reflexively elongates the muscles of the back of your torso.

As it centers, calm, and soothes your brain, the Child's Pose is said to be a beneficial posture for alleviating stress. When done with your head and torso braced, it can as well help relieve back and neck pain.

The Child's Pose soothes the body, mind, and spirit while stimulating your third eye. Gently stretching the lower back, the Child's Pose massages and tones your abdominal organs, and encourages digestion and elimination.

Tip

Before you relax completely, press your palms into the ground with your arms straight and elbows lifted. Push your hips firmly back toward your heels. Breathe deeply into your whole back, for an extra release in your back. Make use of this pose to rest in the middle of more challenging poses.

Corpse Pose (Shavasana)

The Corpse Pose is typically performed at the end of a yoga sequence. It can on the other hand be utilized at the start to calm your body before performing or in the midpoint of a sequence to rest. When applied at the conclusion of a yoga practice it is usually followed by a seated meditation phase to re-incorporate the body mind spirit back into the world.

How to Do

Lying on your back let your arms and legs drop open. With your arms at about forty five degrees from the side of your body, make sure you are comfortable and warm. With your eyes closed begin with slow deep breaths through the nose.

Allowing your entire body to become soft and heavy, let it relax onto the floor. As your body relaxes, feel your full body expanding and decreasing with each breath. Glance over your body from your toes to the top of your head, inspecting for any tension, stiffness or tightened muscles. Intentionally let go and relax any spots that you may find.

Sway or shake those parts of your body from side to side to boost further release.

Let go of all control of your breath, your mind, and your body. Allow your body to move deeper and further into a state of complete relaxation. Remain in the Corpse Pose for five to fifteen minutes.

To release the Corpse Pose gradually deepen your breath, wriggle your fingers and toes, bring your arms over your head and stretch your entire body, breathing out, bend your knees into your chest, then roll over to one side going into the fetal position. Once you are ready, slowly inhaling, rising up into a seated position.

Benefits

The Corpse Pose allows your body and mind the time to sort out what has occurred during a yoga session. To most individuals, no yoga session is finished without this final pose. Your body needs this time to comprehend the new information it has received during the practice of yoga. Even though the Corpse Pose is a resting pose, you are not going to sleep.

Tips

Simply, relax. Follow your breathing without striving to control it. Observe what's taking place in your body. Gather your thoughts as they come along and let them go.

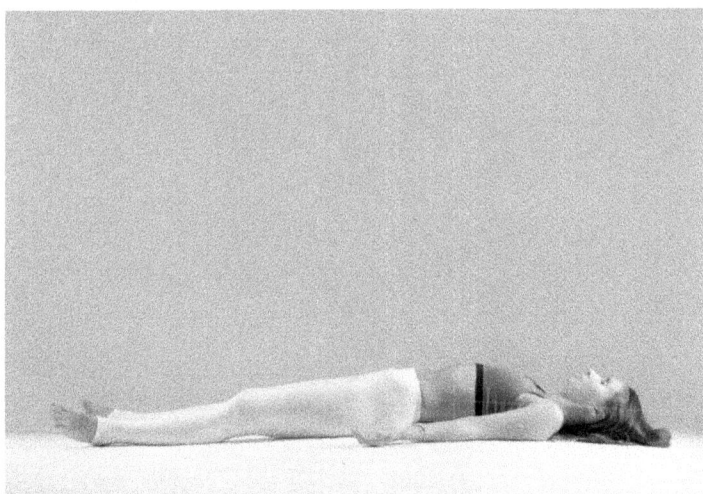

Constructing a Yoga Sequence

Here are a few points to keep in mind how to construct a yoga sequence. You are not at a studio, paying to be there. You do not have to exercise for over an hour. Begin with 5-10 minutes. Notice how you feel by the end of this time. If you feel as if you can do more, go ahead. If no, end your routine there.

Start with 5-10 minutes. By the conclusion of that time, notice how you feel. Do you desire to resume? If yes, continue for an extra five minutes and then check in with yourself once more. If not, close your workout.

The same as any physical journey, a yoga sequence has three clear parts.

Your opening or warm-up sequence

You don't want to jump into the main event tight and cold. This is where you move through and loosening up your major muscle groups as well as body parts

Your main sequence

Once you've warmed up, it's time for your main sequence. This component of your sequence is influenced by the goal of your routine. If it's an asymmetrical pose, keep in mind to do both sides and devote about the same time on each side.

The closing or cool down sequence

Now you've completed the principal portion of your yoga practice, it's time to cool down.

About The Author

Monique Joiner Siedlak is a writer, witch, and warrior on a mission to awaken people to their greatest potential through the power of storytelling infused with mysticism, modern paganism, and new age spirituality. At the young age of 12, she began rigorously studying the fascinating philosophy of Wicca. By the time she was 20, she was self-initiated into the craft, and hasn't looked back ever since. To this day, she has authored over 35 books pertaining to the magick and mysteries of life. Her most recent publication is book one of an Urban Paranormal series entitled "Jaeger Chronicles."

Originally from Long Island, New York, Monique is now a proud inhabitant of Northeast Florida; however, she considers herself to be a citizen of Mother Earth. When she doesn't have a book or pen in hand, she loves exploring new places and learning new things. And being the nature lover that she is, she considers herself to be an avid animal advocate.

To find out more about Monique Joiner Siedlak artistically, spiritually, and personally, feel free to visit her **official website**.

Other Books by Monique Joiner Siedlak

Mojo's Wiccan Series

Wiccan Basics

Candle Magick

Wiccan Spells

Love Spells

Abundance Spells

Hoodoo

Herb Magick

Seven African Powers: The Orishas

Moon Magick

Cooking for the Orishas

Creating Your Own Spells

Body Mind and Soul Series

Creative Visualization

Astral Projection for Beginners

Meditation for Beginners

Reiki for Beginners

Thorne Witch Series

The Phoenix

Beautiful You Series

Creating Your Own Body Butter

Creating Your Own Body Scrub

Creating Your Own Body Spray

Mojo's Self-Improvement Series

Manifesting With the Law of Attraction

Stress Management

Jaeger Chronicles

Glen Cove

Connect With Me!

I really appreciate you reading my book! Please leave a review and let me know your thoughts. Here are the social media locations you can find me at:

Like my Facebook Page: www.facebook.com/mojosiedlak

Follow me on Twitter: www.twitter.com/mojosiedlak

Follow me on Instagram: www.instagram.com/mojosiedlak

Follow me on Bookbub: http://bit.ly/2KEMkqt

Sign up to my Email List at www.mojosiedlak.com and receive a free book!

If you enjoyed this book or found it useful I'd be very grateful if you'd post a short review on at your retailer. Your support really does make a difference and I read all the reviews personally so I can get your feedback and make this as well as the next book even better.

www.ingramcontent.com/pod-product-compliance
Lightning Source LLC
Chambersburg PA
CBHW071619040426
42452CB00009B/1398